Aim High: Astronaut Training

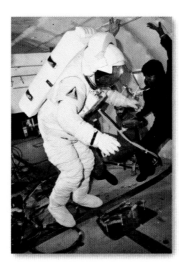

by Donna Longo

PEARSON

Scott Foresman

Editorial Offices: Glenview, Illinois • Parsippany, New Jersey • New York, New York
Sales Offices: Needham, Massachusetts • Duluth, Georgia • Glenview, Illinois
Coppell, Texas • Ontario, California • Mesa, Arizona

Photographs

Every effort has been made to secure permission and provide appropriate credit for photographic material. The publisher deeply regrets any omission and pledges to correct errors called to its attention in subsequent editions.

Unless otherwise acknowledged, all photographs are the property of Pearson Education, Inc.

Photo locators denoted as follows: Top (T), Center (C), Bottom (B), Left (L), Right (R), Background (Bkgd)

Cover (Bkgd) ©Royalty-Free/Corbis; (C) NASA; **1** NASA; 3 NASA; **4** Bettmann/Corbis; **5** DiseÒador/Fotolia; **6** Jack Pfaller/NASA; **7** (BR) ©David Crossland/Alamy Images, (L) RIA Novosti/Alamy Images; **9** JSC/NASA; **10** Keystone Pictures USA/Alamy Images; **11** NASA; **12** ©Associated Press; **13** NASA; **17** (T, B) NASA; **19** NASA; **20** NASA; **21** NASA.

ISBN: 0-328-13568-2

5 6 7 8 9 10 V0B4 18 17 16

Blasting into Space

You have been waiting for this! From your seat on the beach, you watch the space shuttle roar into space. Your family lives near Florida's Cape Canaveral. That's where the launch has taken place. From the beach near your home, you have a great view of the liftoff. You wonder what it would be like to be blasting into space right now.

Onboard the shuttle are seven astronauts from the United States and Russia. Right now, they are headed for the International Space Station (ISS). Upon arrival, they will deliver supplies.

You dream of becoming an astronaut one day. What does it take to become one? What skills do astronauts need? How do they train to go into space? Let's find out!

With a blast, the space shuttle soars into space.

Studying the Skies

Thousands of years ago, people studied the skies. What was their **focus?** They studied the movement of the moon, planets, and stars. The planets seemed to move from place to place. They saw that the moon changed its shape and wondered why.

Today, we know the answers to these questions due to advances in science. On October 4, 1957, the Soviet spacecraft *Sputnik* became the first satellite to travel around Earth. It orbited for three months. During that time, it zipped around the planet every 96 minutes.

A month after *Sputnik's* launch, a dog named Laika became the first living thing in space. In August of 1960, two more dogs, Strelka and Belka, went up too.

The **accomplishments** of Laika, Strelka, and Belka were the start of space travel.

Canine Astronauts Strelka and Belka were sent into space by the Soviets before humans were sent up.

The moon seems to change
shape as it orbits Earth.
We call these changes the
phases of the moon.

The Soviets continued to move forward with space travel. On April 12, 1961, Yuri Gagarin became the first person in space.

At this time, the Soviet Union and the United States did not get along well, and each competed to be better than the other. The United States scrambled to get its own astronauts into space.

Three years earlier, in 1958, the National Aeronautics and Space Administration had been formed. You might know it as NASA. NASA soon began the Mercury program. Its goal was to successfully put a man into orbit around Earth, study his **specific** reactions to living in space, and return him safely again to Earth.

The vehicle assembly building at the Kennedy Space Center in Florida

Cosmonaut Yuri Gagarin was a pilot in the Soviet air force.

Yuri Gagarin orbited Earth in the *Vostok 1.*

The Mercury Astronauts

NASA used military test pilots as their first astronauts. They wanted college graduates with engineering skills. The astronauts had to be the right height and weight too. Why? They had to fit into the close quarters of the space capsule.

On April 9, 1959, NASA introduced the Mercury Seven. This group of men would take on the **role** of space pioneers for the United States.

The Mercury Seven

Alan B. Shepard, Jr.

On May 5, 1961, Alan B. Shepard, Jr., became the first American in space, and also the first to be weightless. On Earth, **gravity** holds us down. It keeps us from floating away. In space, there is so little gravity that people float!

After just 15 minutes in space, Shepard splashed down safely in the Atlantic Ocean.

Shepard's quick flight sent him into space but not into orbit. Now, it was John Glenn's turn to try. On February 20, 1962, Glenn became the first American to orbit Earth. The flight took less than five hours, but Glenn saw both sunrise and sunset! That's because he was zooming around the planet.

Alan B. Shepard was the first American in space.

John Glenn was the first American to orbit Earth.

Footprints on the Moon

On July 20, 1969, millions of people were glued to their TVs. Why? They watched as Neil Armstrong became the first person to walk on the moon. He and Buzz Aldrin had landed the lunar vehicle *Eagle* there. For more than two hours, the men bounced across the moon's dusty surface. They collected rocks, took photos, and did experiments.

What did the men leave behind? Their footprints! Without air to blow them away, the footprints are still there.

An estimated 10,000 people gathered in New York's Central Park to watch giant TV screens and cheer as Neil Armstrong took man's first step on the moon.

Astronaut Training

With today's space shuttle program, NASA looks for two types of astronauts: pilot astronauts and mission specialists. Pilot astronauts are at the vessel's controls. They command the space shuttle. Mission specialists perform tests and **monitor,** or check, any experiments that they are conducting. They send satellites into space and complete repair work. They also go on space walks.

Once astronauts-to-be make it into NASA, they are called astronaut candidates. They go through a year of training. This includes class work, flight training, and survival training.

After the general training ends, it's time for mission training. That's when they practice the jobs they need to do in space. After that, they become astronauts.

Class Work

Astronauts take classes in school just like you. They study the sciences, including physics. That's the study of matter, force, energy, and motion. They also study astronomy, the study of the universe. Astronauts also learn about navigation, or mapping a course from one place to another.

ASTRONAUT CHECKLIST	Pilot Astronaut	Mission Specialist
U.S. citizen	✔	✔
A Bachelor's degree or greater in math, engineering, or physical or biological science	✔	✔
Three years of work experience in an area of study		✔
At least 1,000 hours of flight experience	✔	
Between 5'6" and 6'4" in height	✔	
Between 5' and 6'4" in height		✔
Excellent health	✔	
Very good health		✔
Excellent vision	✔	
Very good vision		✔

Flight Training

Remember, gravity is keeping you from floating away. In space, astronauts work where there is very little gravity. How do astronauts train to work without gravity? They use a special airplane, the KC-135.

The KC-135 climbs high in a curve. Then it suddenly drops, almost two miles down. For 25 seconds, astronauts feel what it's like to be weightless. The climb-and-drop pattern repeats 40 times. Astronauts say that it takes time to get used to it.

Pilot astronauts train with the KC-135 to help them learn to operate a large, heavy aircraft. They also train with the T-38, a much smaller craft.

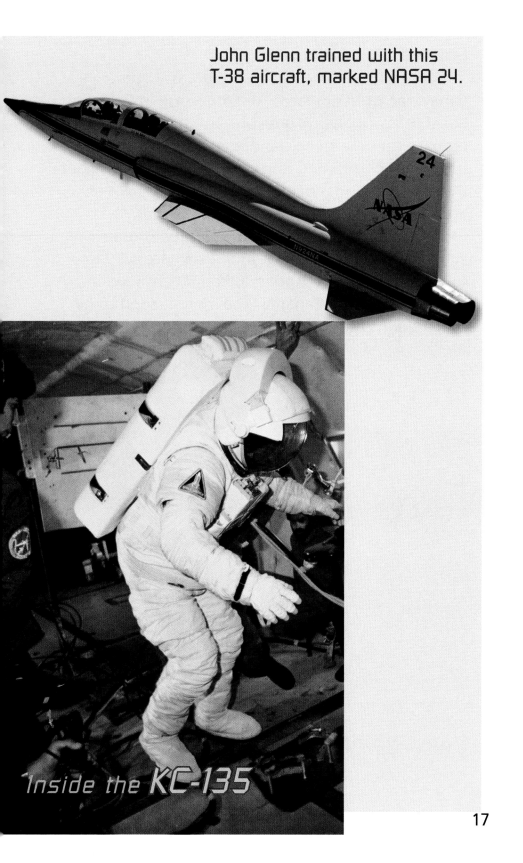

John Glenn trained with this
T-38 aircraft, marked NASA 24.

Inside the *KC-135*

Emergency Landings

Space shuttle landings take place at Cape Canaveral, or at Edwards Air Force Base in California, but that is not always possible. So astronauts must prepare for emergency landings at sea and on other surfaces. One training lesson drags a NASA candidate through water in a parachute harness. It gives an astronaut practice for a parachute landing.

What happens after an astronaut bails out from an emergency situation? It might be necessary to survive on land. The Apollo astronauts trained in the rain forests of Panama. The men needed to be prepared in case they landed in the jungle.

Astronaut Scott Altman simulates an emergency parachute drop into water.

Suiting Up

When astronauts are in orbit, they wear comfortable clothes. They wear sweatpants and T-shirts, just like you! What happens when astronauts work outside the shuttle?

In space, it can be roasting hot in the sunshine or icy cold in the shade. There is no oxygen, and there is always a chance of being hit by space particles. Astronauts cannot survive in space without wearing special spacesuits.

The spacesuit itself has a life-support system. It can keep an astronaut alive for up to eight hours by supplying air. Food and water are stored in the suit, also. There is a headphone and a microphone so an astronaut can stay in touch with others in the shuttle.

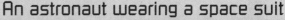

An astronaut wearing a space suit

Living in Space

Living in space comes with special challenges. Astronauts need to sleep, eat, and brush their teeth. The lack of gravity makes these things tricky.

Sally Ride used her background in physics as a *Challenger* mission specialist. She was the first American woman in space. As she got ready to sleep, she had to strap herself down so she didn't float away while dozing off!

Space Food

Space food must be healthy and easy to prepare. Most space food is dehydrated. That means all the water has been taken out of it. To eat it, astronauts just add water. Some foods, such as nuts, fruits, and cereals, are ready to eat.

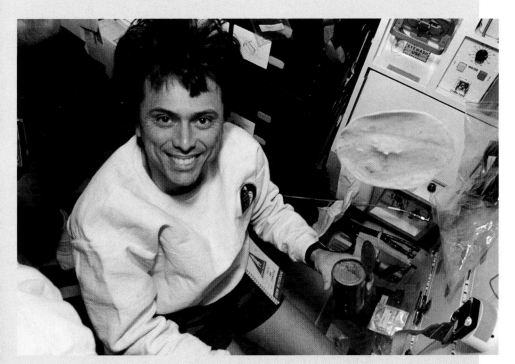

Eating in space

Glossary

accomplishments *n.* successes; achievements; skills.

focus *n.* the central point of attention or activity.

gravity *n.* the force that pulls things toward Earth's center.

monitor *v.* check; keep track of.

role *n.* a purpose or use of someone or something.

specific *adj.* exact; definite.